A Simple Statement

Appomattox Regional Library System
Hopewell, Virginia 23860
11/07

A Simple Statement

A Guide to Nonprofit Arts Management and Leadership

Jamie Grady

HEINEMANN
Portsmouth, NH

Heinemann
A division of Reed Elsevier Inc.
361 Hanover Street
Portsmouth, NH 03801–3912
www.heinemanndrama.com

Offices and agents throughout the world

Library of Congress Cataloging-in-Publication Data
Grady, Jamie
    A simple statement : a guide to nonprofit arts management and
leadership / Jamie Grady.
        p. cm.
    Includes bibliographical references.
    ISBN 0-325-00823-X (alk. paper)
    1. Arts—Management. 2. Nonprofit organizations—Management.
I. Title.
NX760.G72 2006
700'.68—dc22   2005024199

Editor: Lisa A. Barnett
Production: Patricia Adams
Typesetter: Tom Allen/Pear Graphic Design
Cover design: Joni Doherty Design
Manufacturing: Steve Bernier

Printed in the United States of America on acid-free paper
10 09 08 07 06   VP   1 2 3 4 5

To my wife Siouxsie,
without whom there
would be no title

Thank you to my family
and friends,
especially Mildred Kuner
and Cara Grady

Contents

Preface

I began this book with a desire to exude all the information and theories I had learned over the years about arts management and leadership. I started in the summer of 2001, writing pages upon pages of what I believed to be important facts discovered by equally important people. But eventually I realized what I was doing—satisfying my own ego by referencing the many books I had read about nonprofit organizations.

Then I asked a question: What was I trying to say among all the pages of self-pontification? I thought about this question for some time and then realized what I have come to believe in most: the power of the mission statement and the focus of a vision. For me, these two elements are the keys to success for any nonprofit arts institution and are often covered too quickly in nonprofit management books and publications. This is unfortunate because the principles of mission and vision statements run central to our professional and personal lives and can be applied to almost any organizational situation.

Immediately I began to write a mission statement for this book by compiling my values and beliefs, which are as follows:

1. Successful organizational management and leadership can be achieved through simple principles and truths.
2. The creation of new language for old ideas does not constitute an original thought.
3. Useful information on how to run a nonprofit arts organization can be found in an unlimited number of sources.

From these beliefs I produced the following mission statement:

> To provide a book that reveals the universal truths of management and leadership for nonprofit arts organizations in a simplified manner

> To complete this task I will accomplish the following goals:

1. demonstrate how the use of a vision statement and a mission statement runs central to every aspect of a nonprofit arts organization
2. focus on what matters most in leading organizations
3. uncover the common principles that bind our lives in all of our roles
4. reveal the commonality between business and artistic practices

> My vision for this book is as follows:

> To influence an industry.

Now I could begin to gather information for this book based on the criteria of my mission and vision statements. I had thought about and written out my values and beliefs, I had created a mission statement, and I had set down my vision for the final product. I was focused and ready to move forward.

A discussion of nonprofit arts management cannot be conducted in a linear fashion. You cannot move through one definition after another and expect to clearly understand or comprehend the whole. Business principles and concepts tend to be interdependent, and therefore certain ideas must be revisited as new information is brought into the conversation. Think of arts management not so much as a straight line but rather a sphere containing similar but smaller spheres (e.g., fund-raising, marketing, production), each interacting with one another. Information from one sphere is transmitted to a number of other spheres, therefore affecting their actions. It is this type of interaction between organizational units that is at the heart of an arts organization and, for that matter, any type of organization. If you are new to nonprofit arts management, I would encourage you to read this book through at least twice so you may begin to understand the interconnection that exists between an organization's areas of responsibility.

Who Should Read This Book?

This book has the ability to serve a number of audiences. It is an excellent complement to other books about nonprofit arts management and therefore can be used by professors and students in their studies of management in the performing arts and other nonprofit fields. This book can also serve those individuals—staff and board members alike—already in the performing arts field as a reminder of the core principles by which their organizations should be run.

I have written this book based on my experiences in the nonprofit theatre industry. Therefore, the examples given in this book are mainly theatre examples. Instead of giving countless examples of how these principles can be adapted to any of the performing arts fields, I will let readers make those connections for themselves and save a bit of paper and a bit of your time. Much of what is contained in this book can be applied to other arts disciplines and other industries. Because these principles extend beyond the nonprofit sector, anyone interested in management and leadership will find this book applicable to his line of work.

I lay no claim that this will be the only arts management book you will ever need. In particular I have left out much of the how-to information that many other books contain. I encourage you to read those other books and apply the information in those texts to the basic principles of this book. I hope by doing so you will find a new understanding and appreciation for the work you do.

A Simple Statement

Values, Mission, and Vision

1

Organizational Values

T he discussion on nonprofit arts management begins at the very core of every organization— its values. Organizational values are abstract ideas that guide organizational thinking and actions. Organizational values represent the foundation on which the company is formed. They help employees in their decision making and allow them to establish priorities for every aspect of their job. Similarly to organizational values, our personal values inform and shape our own opinions of the way things should work, such as arts education in all elementary schools, greater government support for the arts, and the protection of art by the freedom of speech. We may also share these values with the company in which we work. An organization is, therefore, a collective organism of organizational and personal values.

Defining an organization's unique values is the first and most critical step in its formation and development. "The commitments and beliefs, standards of work and behavior, ways of working, ways of relating to each other, and ways of relating to the community are unique in every successful organization. Everyone involved in an arts organization must understand and share the values or they will not be able to function or contribute to the organization's work" (McDaniel and Thorn 1994, 45–46). If employees within a company do not share beliefs and values similar to those of the organization, they may unintentionally work *against* the values established by the institution. This lack of unity between the organization and its employees will eventually cause a serious disruption in the operational flow of the organization. A group of likeminded people will work more harmoniously than a divergent group. While difference in opinion and skills may be beneficial to the success of an organization, a unity of purpose must be maintained.

In order to understand and identify the values of an organization and to gauge their influence on the company, managers must carefully examine how that organization operates. While it may be helpful to listen to people describe what they believe the values of the organization are, it is far better to observe those people in their day-to-day activities. Note how employees spend their time, how they communicate within the organization, and how they go about their daily job responsibilities and tasks. Although values are often difficult to define, they are usually revealed by employees' actions and thinking, how they set their priorities, and how they allocate their time and energy. An employee's actions are more revealing than her words.

When a company is coming together, its values are derived from its founders—a core group or a single leader. The leader's values regarding the organization, why it is necessary, and how staff members will work within that organization will be transmitted into the corporate culture by the founder's actions. The founder's values will shape the organization and guide it through the formation process. A leader's values often reflect his artistic values and beliefs and the type of work he produces. The leader's values become the foundation upon which the company is formed. However, in order for the institution to achieve success, the values on which the company is built must be appropriate for the time, place, and environment in which the organization will operate. A company's organizational values let others know what it is, why it has been created, and how it is different from other companies.

In their article "Exploring the Impact of Organizational Values and Strategic Orientation on Performance in Not-for-Profit

Professional Theatre," Zannie Giraud Voss and Glenn B. Voss (2000) explore the concept of organizational values and attempt to categorize and articulate some common and more "global" values held in professional nonprofit theatres. They state, "We maintain that the key to firm performance lays in the interaction between basic organizational values—the who we are—and the organization's strategic orientation—the how we operate" (62–63). Through research they uncovered five value dimensions, which are ideal starting points when thinking of an arts organization. The following dimensions help us better understand organizational values and how those values drive an organization:

1. *Prosocial dimension.* Not-for-profit theatres have a responsibility to provide community access to their performances, remove economic and cultural barriers to attendance, and educate audiences in theatre arts.

2. *Market dimension.* Theatres struggle between creating art for art's sake and meeting customer needs and expectations. A purely market-orientated philosophy is typically the mark of a commercial theatre, with its complete reliance on ticket sales for revenues, but all theatre managers recognize the realities of the marketplace.

3. *Financial dimension.* Although all theatres must contend with the reality of financial demands while pursuing creativity and artistic excellence, fiscal stability is a particularly high priority for some theatres.

4. *Achievement dimension.* Public recognition and acclaim can affirm an organization's creative activity, and some theatres particularly strive for external recognition.

5. *Artistic dimension.* For many theatres, the top priority is internally focused creativity, innovation, and artistic independence. (65)

Every nonprofit arts organization is made up of some combination of these five dimensions, in a unique set of proportions according to its own values and beliefs. These values and beliefs influence the organization's corporate culture.

When discussing corporate values, we naturally think of the term *corporate culture*. Corporate culture is the culmination of many factors: the type of business the organization is in, the type of artistic discipline it presents, its programs and services, its audience, its size and location, its methods of operating, and its interaction with the public. Even more important are the intangible factors: beliefs, values, and the norms and expectations of the company. Values play a key role in how an organization operates from day-to-day and how it plans for the future. Values also play a vital role in both the management and the leadership of that company. Therefore, when forming an organization, the founders should evaluate their values to determine if they are appropriate for the present and the future. Changing organizational values will require a substantial effort from the organization's leadership. A change in the company's values will create an operational disruption that could prove costly to the organization. Organizational values must have some sense of timeliness and longevity. Companies that are built upon trends will fail when those trends are no longer fashionable.

An organization is a group of people with specific responsibilities united for a common purpose, and since the values and beliefs of the organization shape its purpose, it is important that the values be articulated formally. An institution may document its values and beliefs through the use of a *statement of beliefs* or *artistic statement.* Regardless of the title an organization chooses for its statement, leadership must fully understand the values that drive the organization and be able to articulate them to others. Without such a statement, employees have no resource for comparing their own values and beliefs with those of the company. The closer the organizational values are to the employee's personal values, the greater the likelihood that the employee will be successful in the organization. In addition, having a clear understanding of a company's values will allow the organization to create the company's mission statement.

The Mission Statement

When founding members of an organization gather together, they might talk about a need they hope to fulfill within a community or the importance of the work of their company. They will talk of the organization's aspirations and dreams and the programs it will generate. These elements are all part of the philosophical foundation of the company, and it is from this idealism that the building blocks of the organization are formed. Nonprofit organizations are formed based upon a philosophical and artistic foundation, which is the by-product of its values and beliefs.

From the philosophical foundation the founders of the organization begin to formulate the mission statement. Creating and documenting mission and vision statements help leaders agree upon the organization's purpose and how it will fulfill its purpose. Effective mission and vision statements create a unifying understanding for anyone who comes in contact with the organization and will provide employees with the proper tools for making day-to-day decisions. The organization's values and beliefs are contained within its mission statement, and employees should be required to embrace that mission.

In Peter F. Drucker's book *Management: Tasks, Responsibilities, Practices* (1974), he states that "to know what a business is we have to start with its purpose. Its purpose must lie outside of the business itself. In fact, it must lie in society since business enterprise is an organ of society. There is only one valid definition of business purpose: to create a customer" (61). Businesses create customers for the values and beliefs that are embedded within their products or services.

How does this apply to arts management? If you start a dance company, not only are you creating art through the organization's presentations, but the organization is also creating an audience for the company, just as Campbell's created an audience for its soups and Microsoft created an audience for its computer software. The products these companies make were once considered unnecessary, but each company sold the values held within its products and ultimately created customers for them. Today, a can of soup can be found in nearly every kitchen, as well as a computer in every home. The final act of an arts organization is to present its art to an audience; the existence of that audience, the customers, cannot be denied. If the organization refuses its audience, it refuses the resources it needs to exist, such as revenues from ticket sales and funding support. Like other companies, arts organizations must find ways to connect the values of their products and services to the values of their potential customers. A mission statement helps an organization articulate, in a concise manner, those possible connections of values and guides the company in its pursuit of its particular audience. The creation of a proper mission statement is the first step to the company's planning process and its successful future.

"Only a clear definition of the mission and purpose of the business makes possible clear and realistic business objectives. It is the foundation for priorities, strategies, plans, and work assignments. It is the starting point for the design of managerial jobs and, above all, for the design of managerial structures" (Drucker 1974, 75). Peter Drucker continues by stating that "the most important single cause of business frustration and business failure" is the lack of attention given to a business' purpose and mission (78). The lack of appreciation for and agreement to an organization's mission has caused considerable disappointment and failure in the non-profit arts field, as well as in the for-profit sector. Too many organizations weaken themselves by reshaping their programming or products to fit outside influences rather than deriving their strength from their original and unique purpose.

The mission statement is the core of every successful organization. A strong and carefully crafted mission statement can identify the extent of operation, facilitate an organization's decision making, communicate an organization's values and priorities, and motivate and unite an organization's stakeholders. Without question, a mission statement is the most important document a nonprofit organization will ever create.

DEFINITION OF A MISSION STATEMENT

A mission statement is a single sentence or short paragraph that states the company's central philosophy, beliefs, values, and principles. It should be recognizable, unique, exciting, and inspiring. It is a simple expression of why the organization was created and what it will accomplish.

Although it communicates grand and lofty ideas, a mission statement should be clear and to the point, consisting of only one to two sentences. Individuals who are not familiar with the organization should be able to quickly and accurately understand its purpose by reading the mission statement. Ambiguity in a mission statement permits individual interpretation, which leads to confusion among stakeholders about the organization's priorities. To avert potential misunderstanding of the mission statement, the organization may add an accompanying paragraph to further define particular words, concepts, or principles. In this respect the mission statement serves as a valuable tool in communicating the organization's philosophy and values. Mission statements should be powerful and compelling in order to bring people together to work toward a common goal. A compelling sense of purpose brings people together to achieve great goals.

If the organization wants every action to be based upon its mission statement, it should create a statement that can be easily memorized. All too often organizations write lengthy mission statements that overwhelm the reader with generalities rather than provide a simple declaration of purpose. A mission statement needs to be brief in order for it to be easily placed in the minds of those who need it most—organizations, employees, patrons, donors, and vendors.

As with any important declaration, it is vital to allow time for revision and discussion about the statement's appropriateness and effectiveness. The creation of the mission statement can be completed by one person or a core group. Usually the statement will be more effective, powerful, and embraced if it is formed by a small group rather than a single person. If the mission statement is developed through a successful group process, each member of that group will have a personal stake in the success of the mission and that of the organization. The more people working toward a focused purpose, and sharing that focus, the greater chance they will have in accomplishing that purpose.

In hard times, when companies experience financial or other difficulties, it is often because they have strayed from the mission of the organization and because organizational values have come into conflict with one another. Over time, companies develop their own culture and that culture may alter with leadership changes, program changes, economic shifts, or other factors. Companies sometimes consciously or unconsciously move away from the original mission or the philosophical foundation. This type of movement creates a confusion of values in the staff, volunteers, audience, and other stakeholders. Often the company in a crisis situation has a number of unstated or assumed priorities that may not be able to work within a single institution.

In times such as these, leadership must look carefully at the organization and determine whether the current mode of operation, its current set of values and beliefs, reflects the current mission statement. If it does not, there are two possible solutions. The first is to reshape the organization to fit the present mission statement and realign the theatre's resources to serve the original vision. The second solution is to adjust the mission statement to fit the current environment of the organization and the beliefs of the organization's current leadership. After all, economic and social environmental changes are inevitable. Creating a new mission statement will help unify the company and refocus people's energies on the strategies of the company. Changing the mission statement changes the organization, however. In effect, the changes create a new company, so this type of reorganization should not be taken lightly. In either case, it is the mission statement that clarifies the work of the organization. The mission statement needs to be the single device with which a company measures its success.

Organizational Goals and Objectives

To help expand upon the mission statement and communicate the direction in which the organization is headed, the founders of an organization will set goals and objectives for the operation. Goals are specific outcomes that an organization seeks to achieve. Goals are set forth to enhance the implementation of the organization's mission (e.g., increase ticket sales). Goals are typically focused on particular programs or services but should also include the infrastructure of the organization—the building, the equipment, human resources—for these resources must be available to the company in order for it to be successful in fulfilling its mission. Organizational infrastructure is often overlooked in planning until it becomes absolutely necessary to take action.

Organizational goals are broken down into objectives. Objectives are measurable accomplishments to be implemented within a specific period of time (e.g., increase single ticket sales by 5% in one season). In this way the goals are aimed at implementing the mission, and the objectives are aimed at attaining the goals. These measurable objectives assist employees in evaluating the company's progress in the short term and allow for operational modifications in order to achieve a desired outcome.

Goals and objectives serve as short-term benchmarks for the organization while it fulfills its mission and moves toward its vision. By establishing goals and a set of measurable objectives, an organization can gauge its success on a day-to-day, month-to-month, and year-to-year basis. Once a company achieves its goals and objectives, leaders set new goals for the organization in alignment with the mission and vision statements.

The use of goals and objectives in a business is a vital part of an ongoing operation. They are the action items through which the mission of a business is carried out, and they articulate the standards against which performance is measured. By establishing goals and objectives, which align with the mission and move toward the organization's vision, an organization sets priorities and determines how resources will be allocated to achieve specific outcomes.

The Vision Statement

Once an organization has rooted itself in a mission statement, it can begin to look toward its future. Leaders must ask: Now that we know who we are, where do we want to go? Where do we want to be in twenty-five years? The answer to these questions form the company's vision. The articulation of that answer is the organization's vision statement.

Visions can come in all shapes and sizes. Individuals can have a vision for themselves, for an organization, or for a society. Whatever the case, a vision statement needs to be challenging, meaningful, and worthy of pursuit. A vision needs to serve as a rallying cry for employees, it must generate excitement, and it must be achievable; otherwise employees would not be motivated to reach the vision. A vision is a picture of the future that people can identify with and believe in. A vision statement clarifies the direction in which an organization is headed. Similarly to the company's values and mission, the organization's vision must be credible and appropriate for the time. A vision statement is the formal documentation of the organization's desired future state of operation, recorded for future use and communication.

DEFINITION OF A VISION STATEMENT

A vision statement is a desired future outcome that is communicated to all organizational stakeholders. It creates a collective focus and demands the attention of the organization's employees. It is a call to action. To achieve its purpose, a vision statement should be

1. Simple, clear, and easily understood. The key element of a strong vision is that it translates complex problems into understandable choices.
2. Distant enough in time to allow for dramatic changes, but close enough to gain commitment from the organization. The vision must be realistic and credible. The vision must also create a sense of urgency.
3. [Designed to] focus the organization on the right things, particularly the things it does best.
4. Frequently articulated by top management to gain solid consensus that the vision is desirable and achievable. The CEO must personify the vision and live by it. The vision must challenge the entire organization. (Rowe et al. 1986, 58)

Similar to the mission statement, a vision statement should be brief. In this case it should be one sentence or less. It is the company's rallying cry. It is the symbolic representation of what the organization hopes to achieve in the future and how the organization will be affected by this change. It is the collective and distinct aspirations of a group of people who share similar values and beliefs and are guided by a central purpose.

Organizational Focus

The great power of a vision statement lies in its ability to focus an organization on a future desired outcome. The vision statement can be used by every employee as a litmus test for all decisions. The question that everyone in the organization should be asking herself is: Will this positively affect the company's advancement toward the vision statement? If the answer is yes then the employee must act. If the answer is no then the employee must move on to the next task or question. A vision statement and a mission statement are extremely useful in sorting through information and determining what is and is not important to the organization. They help organize the company's priorities.

In stage director William Ball's book *A Sense of Direction*, he describes his process of using "metaphors" to help guide his work. He states:

> When preparing a new production, I usually ask a director to find a photograph or a painting that most clearly symbolizes to him the entire concept of the play. Then I ask him to limit the production of the play to the colors, the textures, and the tone of that picture. . . . This limitation is creative. Its great advantage is that it keeps out a lot of extraneous and unmatched ingredients. The discipline of following one *metaphor* requires the director to unify his thoughts.
>
> Exercising great discipline in conforming to one *metaphor* tends to give the production visual unity, consistency, and power. Without a *metaphor*, one is working at random with unlimited resources of color, line, texture. In such productions, the fact that the ingredients are unlimited causes the work to look like a shamble of accidents. Since we seek unity in a work of art, there is a great advantage in using a device that forces unity into the production. There should be only one *metaphor*. . . . More than one *metaphor* would be immediately confusing and disunifying. (1984, 34–35)

The use of a metaphor is an excellent way for an organization's leader to relate a vision. As a leader of a theatrical production, Ball establishes a vision for the production, which everyone can understand and work toward achieving. Unity of thought in a single production or within an organization requires that everyone in the group understands the collective desired outcome. Everything else becomes unimportant. Vision statements focus the energies and resources of the organization on the right results and provide organizational focus, unity, consistency, and power.

Getting the Most Out of Your Mission and Vision Statements

COMMUNICATE! COMMUNICATE! COMMUNICATE!

Great mission and vision statements are useless if people never read or hear them. The statements should have the capacity to speak to all of the organization's stakeholders and should be constantly displayed and voiced. Mission and vision statements should be placed on company letterhead, business cards, brochures, posters, solicitation letters, and anything else that is viewed by the staff and the public. This public display ensures that all of the stakeholders of the organization understand the fundamental purpose of the organization and can take the proper actions to help fulfill that mission.

BUILDING A SHARED VISION

Organizational success requires the ability to communicate a compelling image of the future that induces enthusiasm and commitment from the staff and consumers. Once a vision statement for an organization has been established, either through an individual or group process, it is the duty of the leader to share that vision with the rest of the organization and to build a coalition of support for it. Leaders should use every vehicle possible to communicate the vision and strategies of the organization to all stakeholders.

Communication should not be limited to words. Leaders may communicate a vision through images, metaphors, music, stories, and sounds. Whatever it takes to reinforce and secure a common vision is the right communication tool. The mission and vision statements can be communicated through the language used in brochures, in individual marketing pieces, and in fund-raising materials. Because managers and trustees of nonprofit organizations make decisions based upon the mission and vision statements, the statements should be included at the top of all meeting agendas. The vision statement can be displayed in the office entry to motivate employees, and it should live in the heart and mind of everyone who comes in contact with the organization.

Limit the organization's vision statement to as few words as possible so it can become the organization's logo, motto, or rallying cry. It should be used at every opportunity to remind the staff of the purpose of their work—to remind them of what they have agreed is the desired outcome.

MOTIVATING ACTION

Communicating the vision statement is not about telling people what the company wants of them; it is about showing people what they want. It is human nature for employees to be more interested in getting what they want rather than in working toward what the company wants. This is why it is important that vision statements instill in employees a personal desire and empower them to share and participate in the organization's future. It is not enough to talk about the vision statement to employees; leaders must explain how obtaining this desired outcome would benefit them professionally and personally. What will be their rewards?

True leaders are aware that they cannot do everything themselves. By sharing a vision of the future, they empower others within the organization to assume responsibility and authority. Through the communication of a vision statement, leaders instill in others a fundamental and collective grand goal. A vision statement aligns the energies of a group toward a single purpose and allows other leaders to emerge in the pursuit of that outcome. Empowered employees make the right decisions and work hard to bring the organization's vision to fruition.

MEASURE OF SUCCESS

For a nonprofit organization, making a profit is not necessarily the definitive measure of success, nor is an increased budget size or staff. The evaluation of success lies in the mission and vision statements and is particular to that organization. Success may represent an increase in audience, in the number of people served by a particular program, or in artistic quality. Success is also measured by the progress the company has made in fulfilling its vision. Success is measured in the short term by the accomplishment of goals and objectives and how those accomplishments have moved the organization closer to its vision. Vision statements give the organization and its employees an image of success. Without the need to succeed, people and organizations would never reach their full potential. Reaching the company's full potential is what a vision statement is all about.

EVALUATE AND REVIEW

What I have described in this chapter is very similar to the process of strategic planning. At the beginning of an organization's history, planning will take place so the company can see itself in the next three to five years and perhaps even beyond. This planning will give those involved an understanding of what their efforts are moving toward. And as with any planning process, those plans must be reviewed annually. The staff and board of a nonprofit arts organization should review the mission and vision statements each year to determine whether their purpose is still relevant to the current environment. Business environments change, and so do organizations. A change in leadership, community demographics, the economy, or technology can affect the way an organization sees itself and conducts its business. It is important for the staff and board of trustees to recognize this change and document it properly in the mission and vision statements.

The importance of a clearly defined organization cannot be stressed enough. Such an organization includes a strong vision statement, a clear and powerful mission statement, and properly thought-out and articulated goals and objectives. It also includes the necessary complementary materials, which help to define clearly the work of the organization and its values. These elements are the fundamental starting point on which the rest of the organization will be built. If the foundation is weak, sooner or later the organization will collapse on itself.

In organizations, values define the mission, the mission determines goals, and goals are broken down into objectives, all of which work toward fulfilling the vision. The following chapters will explore how these basic elements affect the management and leadership of every function within a nonprofit performing arts organization.

The following is an excellent example of the use of a vision statement, a mission statement, and a statement of values to clearly communicate the philosophical foundation of an arts organization to its stakeholders.

COURT THEATRE—STRATEGIC PLAN (1997/98–2001/02 SEASONS)

Mission ▪ Court Theatre exists to celebrate the immutable power and relevance of classic theatre.

Vision ▪ We share a collective aspiration to create a National Center for Classic Theatre.

Strategic Decisions Are Guided by the Following Statement of Values

1. We believe theatre satisfies an innate human need for communal acts of imagining.
2. We believe works for the stage that reveal timeless themes and illuminate universal truths are classics.
3. We believe in the primacy of language in theatre.
4. We believe in an artistic aesthetic that is provocative, emotive, disciplined, and irreverent.
5. We believe in an artistic process that is venturous, collaborative, grounded in thorough research and dynamically evolving.
6. We believe an environment of trust, generosity, and shared vision enables risk-taking in the artistic process.
7. We believe the artistic process should inform all aspects of the theatre's operations including leadership, governance, and administration.

8. We believe classic theatre is a vital participant in American culture, its survival and maturation.

9. We believe artists make significant contributions to their communities.

10. We believe learning is a life-long journey, and classic theatre has a unique ability to teach and inspire its creators and patrons.

11. We believe in freedom of expression, and embrace a plethora of artistic voices and styles.

12. We believe in diversity across all definitions. (From www.courttheatre.org)

The Basics of Forming a Nonprofit Organization

2

A s an organization's programs and services begin to take shape and its short-term goals and objectives are drafted, it should begin the process of incorporation. This is done in tandem with the development of the mission and vision statements. The incorporation process is the formal recognition of the organization as a legal business entity with all the related privileges and responsibilities. At this time, the nonprofit organization should also begin to identify a small number of potential board members.

Legally Forming a Nonprofit Corporation

The best advice I can give to those forming a nonprofit organization is to obtain legal counsel. The process of state incorporation and filing for federal tax exemption can be long and complicated. Good legal counsel will help the organization avoid costly mistakes and prevent unnecessary legal issues from arising in the future. As a nonprofit organization, it is important to maintain proper legal standing.

While the Internet and other resources can be extremely valuable during this process, a legal adviser should be the one to guide the organization step-by-step through the procedure. In addition to the Internet, other resources can be used for informational purposes and to help prepare the organization for the task ahead. It is wise to be aware of the process and knowledgeable enough to know when to ask for help. Many attorneys will assist nonprofit organizations on a pro bono basis. Local arts councils and other nonprofit organizations may be able to direct the company to an experienced attorney who will work with the organization for free or at a reduced rate.

Special Considerations for Forming a Nonprofit Corporation

A corporation is a legal entity that has been formed for a particular purpose, which can have either a for-profit or nonprofit motive. A corporation is treated as a separate entity distinct from the people who own, manage, oversee, or work within it. As a corporation, the business operates under certain state and federal laws and regulations. Many of these rules and regulations are concerned with tax collection, employment practices, and financial accounting standards. Most organizations file for incorporation for liability protection. Under normal conditions liability protection shelters trustees, manager, and employees from being held personally liable for corporate debts and liabilities.

Differences Between For-Profit and Nonprofit Organizations

In order for an organization to be recognized by state and federal agencies as an ongoing concern, it should file for incorporation. Should an arts organization automatically incorporate as a nonprofit organization? The differences between a for-profit organization and a nonprofit organization are sometimes overlooked. Perhaps, particularly in the performing arts, it may be advisable to incorporate as a for-profit company rather than a nonprofit one. The advice of a certified public accountant (CPA) or other financial consultant might help clarify this decision. Unlike a for-profit corporation, a nonprofit corporation can collect financial gifts from individuals, businesses, foundations, and government agencies as well as receive tax-exemption benefits. These differences are usually enough to satisfy one's desire to incorporate as a nonprofit corporation. However, the mission of the organization may indicate a for-profit motive, even though the company has been established to produce art. There are many for-profit organizations in this country producing art on a commercial level. It is important to consider the pros and cons of incorporating the organization as either a for-profit or nonprofit company and make the appropriate decision for the organization. It is a decision that should not be taken lightly.

The following criteria distinguish a for-profit corporation from a nonprofit corporation:

1. Nonprofit corporations generally cannot issue shares or pay dividends; nonprofit corporations can make a profit, but it must be returned to the company.
2. Nonprofit corporations' primary activity must be compliant with federal tax-exemption laws.
3. Nonprofit organizations must not make a substantial amount of income from an activity other than as stated within its mission.

This last distinction is the most important. By filing for tax-exempt status, the organization is declaring that it will serve a public good, which is its primary purpose. Most other activities would be considered "unrelated" to its nonprofit purpose. An exempt corporation may be subject to a tax on unrelated business income (UBI) if it operates a business that is unrelated to its exempt purpose. If its unrelated business activities are significant, the corporation could lose its exemption status. The U.S. Internal Revenue Service (IRS) tax code for unrelated business tax income (UBTI) excludes dividends, interest, royalties, most rents, insubstantial rent, capital gains, and certain research income. For this reason each organization should consider the methods of how it will generate its revenue to determine if those methods fall under a for-profit or nonprofit business model.

Under federal regulations a recognized nonprofit tax-exempt company is entitled to certain benefits. These benefits include the following:

1. *Exemption from federal and state tax.* Nonprofit corporations are eligible for state and federal exemptions from payment of corporate taxes, as well as other tax exemptions and benefits.

2. *Public and private funding.* Nonprofit corporations are eligible to receive both public and private grants and contributions.

3. *Annuity programs for employees.* Employees of nonprofit companies may take advantage of certain special tax-sheltered annuities. Such plans differ from standard IRA plans in that employees may be able withdraw funds without tax penalty under certain conditions.

4. *Other benefits.* Benefits include lower postal rates on third-class bulk mailings and the availability of public service announcements on radio and television and newspapers.

Bylaws

Once the organization has filed all of the necessary paperwork and has received its certificate of incorporation from the state in which it will be conducting its business, the board should meet to adopt its bylaws. Bylaws usually do not have to be filed with state incorporation applications or be approved by government agencies. They do, however, have to be submitted along with the organization's federal application for tax exemption. This does not lessen the importance of a well-crafted set of bylaws.

An organization's bylaws are a written document that governs the operation of the board of directors and should reflect the board's responsibility to the organization. Bylaws are the rules that guide the actions and procedures of the board. The document should contain rules for the conduct of officers and board members, a statement of their duties, and a description of committee structure. The construction of the company's bylaws should be guided by the mission and vision of that organization. The values and beliefs that are embedded within the mission and vision statements should also determine how the board operates in relation to the organization and the general public.

Bylaws should not be drawn up as a means to satisfy the current needs of the organization; rather, they should be written in a way that will satisfy the organization's needs in the future. When establishing bylaws, one should think of the organization several years out and consider how the organization would best be served by the board of trustees. What problems or needs might be addressed in the bylaws in order to head off potential organizational conflict? When developing an organization's bylaws, it might be wise to ask for a copy of the bylaws from a few other organizations that have a similar mission in order to compare how those organizations were formed. It would also be beneficial to talk with the directors of other similar organizations and to consult legal counsel. The bylaws of other similar organizations may be of help in crafting a set of bylaws for your organization, but you should refrain from simply copying them word for word. What makes your organization unique, as stated in the mission statement, will dictate differences in board structure. Organizational bylaws will continue to be examined in the following chapter, on the board of trustees.

The Board of Trustees 3

W hen organizing an institution's board of trustees, it's important to realize that there is no one way to construct or manage a board. Every organization must evaluate its mission and vision statements to determine the unique roles and responsibilities that it will ask of its board members. The responsibilities of the board should be developed to best serve the mission and values of the organization. The board and its operating bylaws should create a collective focus and purpose for the whole organization.

A great deal of confusion has surrounded the role of a board in both for-profit and nonprofit organizations. This confusion has been created by the inherent conflict between what the law states regarding the function of boards and managers' expectations of how boards should operate. It is a continuing battle between fact and fiction. Unfortunately, state laws regarding boards are ambiguous, which has only added to the confusion.

In general terms, a board is the governing body of the corporation. The board is responsible for overseeing the organization through the evaluation and implementation of corporate policy. A board will review the organization to ensure that it is operating ethically and within the law. However, it is not responsible for the day-to-day management of the organization. In these ways the boards of for-profit and nonprofit organizations function very similarly. To distinguish between the two groups, companies generally call a for-profit board a board of directors and a nonprofit board a board of trustees.

Great effort and care should be taken when establishing the board and selecting its initial members. The board of trustees in a nonprofit organization sets the tone for the entire organization, and once a particular board structure is in place it is extremely difficult to change. Inexperienced managers who rush to emulate traditional models of trusteeship often end up with a dysfunctional governing body. A board that lacks a sense of the organization's mission and values can lead to unending deadlock and organizational confusion.

In the 1960s, when funding for the arts was plentiful, arts boards were not required to provide the same type of leadership as they are today, nor did they need to. An improperly run board was of little importance when organizations were operating smoothly, contributed income was abundant, and organizations' budgets were growing. But in the twenty-first century, funding dollars have shifted away from the arts, and competition for the remaining pool has become more intense. This pressure has caused many nonprofit organizations to reexamine the role of their board and how it functions in respect to support of the organization.

During the start-up phase of an arts organization, the board is often looked upon as a source of financial support as well as a source of volunteer person-hours. During this period board members are deeply connected to the day-to-day operation of the organization through their volunteerism. As the number of full-time employees increases, however, the role of the board changes and the need for their volunteer labor becomes less important to the organization. This shift in structure can cause considerable confusion with board members who no longer feel involved in the organization, and bitterness in the executives who resent the board's attempts to micromanage the organization. As with any serious problem in board operations, once this type of dysfunction exists within an organization, it is difficult and time-consuming to correct. When forming the board, it is important to think not of what the organization needs today but what it will need in the future. It is also important to choose members who will understand and be able to handle the gradual shift in responsibilities as the organization grows.

Examining State Law

In order to fully understand the role of the board, discussion must begin with state law. Throughout this section, I will reference the Not-for-Profit Corporation Law of New York State. Section 701(a) of the law states, "Except as other wise provided in the certificate of incorporation, a corporation is managed by the board of directors." Paragraph (b) states, "If the certificate of incorporation vests the management of the corporation, in whole or in part, in one or more persons other than the board, individually or collectively, such other person or persons shall be subject to the same obligations and the same liabilities for managerial acts or omissions as are imposed upon directors by this chapter" (New York State Legislature n.d.). As described within the law, the board has the option of managing the corporation or handing over the responsibility of management to another individual or individuals. If they choose the latter, as they normally do, then what becomes the responsibility of the board? It must oversee the person(s) in charge of managing the corporation.

This is the first decision an organization has to make regarding its board: is it appropriate for the board to manage the organization, or should the board assign another person or persons with that responsibility? In many instances the mission statement will guide the company in this decision. Board members of an organization that is volunteer based may decide to hold on to management responsibilities rather than assign a staff person as manager and thus change the makeup of the organization. In most cases when a professional organization is needed to fulfill the mission, the board will assign day-to-day responsibilities to another person, therefore transferring its power from management to oversight.

Further analysis of state law will reveal other factors for organizations to consider when forming a board of trustees. For example, in order for a board to be considered legal in accordance with New York State law, it must meet the following conditions:

1. Each director shall be at least eighteen years of age . . . ;
2. The number of directors constituting the entire board shall be not less than three (president, secretary, treasurer);
3. Directors and officers shall discharge the duties of their respective positions in good faith and with that degree of diligence, care, and skill which ordinarily prudent men would exercise under similar circumstances in like positions;
4. The certificate of incorporation or the by-laws may prescribe other qualifications for directors . . . ; [and]
5. (a) Meetings of members may be held at such place, within or without this state, as may be fixed by or under the by-laws or, if not so fixed, at the office of the corporation in this state. (b) A meeting of the members shall be held annually for the election of directors and the transaction of other business on a date fixed by or under the by-laws. (New York State Legislature n.d., Article 7 Not-For-Profit Corporation)

As the previous section highlights, the responsibilities of the board of trustees are not completely dictated by the state and federal governments. The duties and responsibilities of board members are regulated by the organization's bylaws.

The question is not: What does the board do for the organization? But rather: What *should* the board do for the organization? Perhaps an equally valid question is: What does the organization want the board *not* to do? How can the board of trustees be structured and operate to best serve the mission and vision of the organization? Through the exploration of these questions, the organization can construct its bylaws and vote board members into office.

The Responsibilities of Nonprofit Boards

The responsibilities of a nonprofit board are as follows:

- ensure adequate resources for the organization to fulfill its mission through fund-raising and marketing activities
- serve as community spokespeople, articulating the organization's values, mission, and vision
- recruit, train, and evaluate board members to ensure future trusteeship
- oversee the work of the executive staff, including:
    review the organization's mission, programs, policies, and vision
    monitor fiscal activity of the organization and establish necessary fiscal policies
    hire, evaluate, support, and terminate executive staff members
    ensure effective long-term strategic planning for the organization
    ensure the provisions of the law are being followed

Each of these areas represents a critical function in the role of board governance and is fully described in this chapter.

ENSURE ADEQUATE RESOURCES FOR THE ORGANIZATION TO FULFILL ITS MISSION

Nonprofit organizations rely on their board of trustees as a source of support. Support can come in many forms, such as advice and counsel, access to key community members, public relations, and earned and unearned financial support. Board members should be a reliable source of contributed revenue for the organization. They should contribute money directly to the organization and should seek out donations from their peers as well as from their professional contacts. In addition, board members should purchase tickets to all of the organization's events and actively promote the events being presented by the organization.

SERVE AS COMMUNITY SPOKESPEOPLE

It seems only natural that as firm believers in the values, mission, and vision of the organization as well as in the importance of the organization within a given community, board members would make ideal spokespeople for the organization. It is always helpful for an organization to have people in the community pulling for them and promoting their mission, whether they are talking with friends or colleagues, in a business or community setting.

RECRUIT, TRAIN, AND EVALUATE BOARD MEMBERS

Because state law requires that organizations maintain at least three members on their board, it seems evident that one of its responsibilities is to satisfy this minimum requirement. Boards are responsible for recruiting new board members, a vital and continuous function. With larger boards, a nominating committee should be formed to identify and select potential new board members. Before considering any other classifications such as professional status, area of expertise, sex, race, and position in community, trustees need to bear in mind that potential board members should already share a common sense of values and contribute to the organization. Nothing less will do. The board is not the appropriate place to educate individuals about the organization.

Board recruitment can be as daunting and challenging as hiring the executive staff. Board recruitment is the process of identifying and enlisting members of the community who share similar values as those of the organization. Performing arts groups are fortunate to have potential board members waiting for them in the audience. After all, one of the reasons people regularly attend arts events is because they share the same values as the organization. Many of these patrons also donate money to the organization. Already they have met two of the requirements for board members: they share the organizational values and mission, and they help provide the necessary resources through financial contributions.

OVERSEE THE WORK OF THE EXECUTIVE STAFF

When a board elects to transfer the management of the corporation to another individual or individuals, it turns over the right to make day-to-day decisions. Instead the members focus their attention on overseeing the performance of the executive staff to ensure the organization is run properly. As such a body, the board will be engaged in the following activities.

Reviewing the Organization's Mission, Programs, Policies, and Vision ▪ The mission statement of a nonprofit organization is typically formulated by the founding members of that company. The board is not usually responsible for creating a mission statement but rather for reviewing it to ensure that the organization is operating under its original charter as filed with state and federal government agencies. In addition, the board must similarly review the organization's programs and policies to ensure the fulfillment of the vision.

Board members must fully understand that the mission and vision statements represent the philosophical foundation of the organization and are the driving and defining elements in all decisions and relationships. The combination of values, mission, vision, and leadership make the organization unique. Regular review of these statements is essential to the continued focus of the organization and ultimately to its success.

Monitoring Fiscal Activity of the Organization and Establishing Necessary Fiscal Policies ▪ As part of its fiscal responsibilities, the board must continually monitor and evaluate the financial activity of the organization and determine fiscal policy that best suits the organization and ensures accountability of its staff members. During board meetings the treasurer will report to the full board on the ongoing financial concerns of the organization. Often the treasurer will distribute a variety of financial statements to inform the board about where the organization is in regard to its original budget as well as the organization's assets and liabilities.

At the end of each fiscal year an independent auditor should be brought in to conduct a financial review of the organization and report the results to the board. Independent audits are an excellent way to check the work of staff members and to ensure the organization is following all federal and state accounting standards and practices.

In addition to approving the annual budget, board members will also make decisions on investment options, long-term debt management, and other significant financial matters. The effectiveness of their decision-making process is enhanced by each board member's understanding of the financial information presented. Often board members are asked to vote on issues that will have a significant effect on the organization, but they have very little understanding of the information that is being presented. Board members must be continually trained and educated in the understanding of important financial documents and the decision-making process in order to make the best possible decisions for the organization. This responsibility rests not only with the board president but also with the board treasurer and the executive staff.

Hire, Evaluate, Support, and Terminate Executive Staff Members ▪ Since the board of trustees oversees the executive staff, it has the responsibility of hiring, evaluating, supporting, and possibly terminating the employment of the executive director and/or the artistic director.

The hiring of executive staff can be a lengthy and demanding process. Often a number of seemingly qualified candidates will appear to have very little in common with one another, but each candidate may have the potential to benefit the company. In such situations the board must try to identify the candidate that most closely matches the organization's values, mission, and vision. Hiring a candidate who does not share the same values as the company will only create confusion and set up a greater likelihood of failure for the new hire. All too often, when it is time to hire new leadership, the board of trustees sees this as an opportunity to change directions rather than strengthen the organization's current position.

Equally important to hiring the right candidate for the organization is the board's responsibility of executive evaluation. It is essential that each year the board of trustees evaluates the performance of the executive staff. Performance evaluation should be based upon how well the employee upholds the values and mission of the organization and how successfully the organization has moved toward fulfilling its vision. Staff evaluation should not be regarded negatively but rather as an opportunity to support staff and to clarify organizational goals. Executive-level turnover can be costly to an organization and good executive-level employees are hard to find. Their strengths and weaknesses need to be identified and addressed by the board. Upper-level managers needs to know how they are doing and where they stand with the board. However, if an executive staff member is not meeting the expectations of the board of trustees, then the board must terminate that employee and seek out a suitable replacement.

Ensure Effective Long-Term Strategic Planning for the Organization ▪ The role of the board of trustees is not day-to-day management. Professional staff, who have educational training and experience in their areas, are hired to fulfill the day-to-day needs of the organization. Board members may be called upon for advice and opinions on certain matters, but ultimately it is each staff person's responsibility to run his or her department. What boards are responsible for, with the involvement of executive staff members, is developing long-range plans that align with the organization's vision and the manner in which the organization will reach this goal. For example, the board should focus on decisions pertaining to long-term financial investments, capital campaigns and construction, and personnel benefits policies.

Ensure the Provisions of the Law Are Being Followed ▪ The board of trustees of a nonprofit organization must uphold the law regarding nonprofit entities. Legal matters pertaining to a nonprofit organization can include tax liabilities, tax-filing procedures, board procedures, and employment practices, to name just a few. Board members should periodically review the organization's policies to ensure legal compliance.

In addition to these responsibilities, board members are often required by the organization to perform other duties as part of their service to the organization. They are expected to attend meetings, purchase tickets to productions, and attend special events. Whatever the responsibilities of the board members are, they should be in agreement with the mission and values of the organization.

Board Members as Volunteers Versus Leaders

What makes the relationship between the board and the organization interesting, complex, and confusing is the fact that board members are volunteers. Boards of directors in the for-profit environment are compensated to oversee the operations of organizations. Compensation sets up a clear sense of duty for these individuals—to oversee and advise the operation. The board of directors has a responsibility to the company's shareholders.

Board members of nonprofit organizations, however, do not get paid for their service on the board and are therefore volunteers. The board of trustees has a responsibility to the community and the organization it has been entrusted to oversee. Because the board members are volunteers, the paid staff needs to take responsibility for directing, managing, and supporting the work of the board. The staff must focus the board's energy toward generating resources for the organization, promoting the organization and its mission to the community, and maintaining its own existence (i.e., nominating, reporting, etc.). In this way board members function very much like other volunteer groups within the organization.

Since the board is a group of volunteers who have come to assist the organization, the executive staff must play an active role in the board's development, knowledge, and actions as it would with any volunteer group. When discussing the long-term goals of an organization or when solving critical issues, however, the board members should serve as leaders of the organization. When making long-term planning decisions, the board should listen to all parties and, in particular, to the advice of the professional staff. As leaders of the organization, board members help shape the direction in which the company is headed. This planning must agree with the mission and vision of the organization and must be appropriate for the community. Under ideal conditions, where everyone is firmly rooted in the organization's values and mission, everyone will share similar long-term goals. A disjointed understanding or commitment to the values and mission of the organization will undoubtedly create conflict when deciding upon long-term strategies.

When a nonprofit organization is met with a crisis situation, the board must spring into action and firmly assume the role of leader. Often this occurs when the organization is without executive staff, when the organization is faced with a serious financial crisis, or when the effectiveness of the executive staff is in question. When the organization's existence is at stake, it is the responsibility of the board to correct the situation. This could mean firing the executive staff or other key staff members, bringing in an outside consultant or auditor, raising funds to cover debt, or refinancing that debt to continue operations. It could also require that the organization cease to operate.

The challenge with this system is creating the proper balance between volunteerism and leadership. Some boards operate strictly under the volunteer model and fail to assume their leadership role when most needed. The other extreme is the board that assumes ultimate leadership and micromanages the operation. Neither of these boards is very effective. There must be a balanced approach to board involvement in the organization.

Many people are confused about the role of a board of trustees. In fact, the terms *board of directors* and *board of trustees* are sometimes used interchangeably when describing nonprofit boards. The term *trustee* is associated with volunteerism and the word *director* with leadership. At all times a board of trustees is operating on a seesaw of authority and oversight. If the organization is strong and operating smoothly, then the board members will serve more as volunteers, helping to continue the organization's prosperity while keeping an eye on the whole as trustees. When the organization is in crisis, board members must act as directors and exercise their leadership privilege and obligation to set the organization back on track.

Bylaws Revisited

Now that we have established a clear understanding of the role and responsibilities of the board of trustees, it is appropriate to revisit the function of the organization's bylaws. Again, bylaws are the rules and regulations under which the board of trustees operate. Bylaws typically address the following issues:

- board size
- board member meetings

- committee structure, including:
    executive committee
    finance committee
    nominating committee

Each of these areas is explored in relationship to mission and vision statements in the following sections.

BOARD SIZE

The size and scope of the board should always be set in relationship to the size and complexity of the organization as well as the size and responsibility of the professional staff. Each organization has to determine what is the appropriate size and structure for that particular organization. The result is an individual entity whose makeup and size are unique to its mission.

However, the size of the board is not as important as the board's effectiveness in fulfilling its responsibilities. A small board of committed, focused people can be as effective, if not more effective, than a large, disorganized group. The legal minimum number of a board of trustees is three people over the age of eighteen (president, treasurer, and secretary). For organizations that are just beginning, this minimum number seems ideal. Once the company begins operation in earnest and is presenting events to the public, staff and board members can explore the roster of patrons to determine if any of them would be ideal candidates for board membership. Ideal candidates are patrons who demonstrate a belief in the values and mission of the organization and have a predisposition to contribute to the organization. It would be a mistake for a new organization to fill its board with members for the sake of having a large body of trustees instead of waiting for the right people to make themselves known to the group, which they eventually will.

As the organization grows, so too can the board. However, the effectiveness of the board depends on the support and direction of the staff and the amount of time they can appropriate to the board. Theoretically, the more support and direction a board receives from the staff, the more effective the board will be and the more successful the organization will be (i.e., the more resources will be garnered in support of the organization's programs). Staff members must understand that the board has a responsibility to provide resources to the organization, but the staff has the responsibility to motivate the board members and provide them with the tools necessary to be successful in their task. As board size increases, so too must the time the staff dedicates to board operations.

Often bylaws state the minimum and maximum number of board members that can serve on the board at a given time. The minimum number of board members is set by state law, but it seems unnecessary that a maximum number of board members be stated because the size of the board is often proportional to the size of the organization. Not stating a maximum number of board members will allow the organization's trusteeship to alter appropriately with the size of the organization.

BOARD MEMBER MEETINGS

State law requires that boards meet at least once a year. This meeting is appropriately called the annual meeting. The annual meeting should focus on the tasks that the board needs to accomplish. These tasks include financial and policy review, voting in new officers and members, budget approval, resource procurement, and long-term planning.

More commonly, boards have monthly information-sharing meetings where staff members and committee chairs report to the entire board. Another option that might be as effective as meetings is to prepare emails or monthly reports for the board members. Of course there are pros and cons for both of these methods. Still, not all board meetings need to be agenda or information driven. Board meetings can serve as brainstorming sessions for areas such as season selection, fund-raising, and marketing; after all, the board of trustees is a part of your audience. Board meetings might be used to survey board members about program outcomes or long-term planning. Board meetings might also be used as training sessions, which help to strengthen the work and commitment of the group. Under any meeting structure, the staff must respect the time being given by the board members. If board members attend too many unproductive meetings, they could lose focus on the organization. If smaller committees are meeting on a more regular basis (e.g., monthly or biweekly), full board meetings become an additional and perhaps even unwelcome burden to members with already demanding schedules. When determining the frequency of board meetings, ask: What is the most effective way to accomplish the goals and tasks of the board? How can the organization keep the board engaged and positive? How can the board fulfill its responsibilities while respecting everyone's time?

COMMITTEE STRUCTURE

In order to work more efficiently, a large board is typically broken down into smaller groups, which are assigned more defined tasks. The following three committees typically exist within a board: executive, finance, and nominating.

The *executive committee* is composed of the chair or president, the vice chair or vice president, the treasurer, and the secretary. This committee is empowered to act on behalf of the full board when a situation requires immediate action and the gathering of the full board is impossible. The executive committee should meet on an ad hoc basis to resolve important and urgent issues. Executive committees should refrain from meeting on a regular basis to avoid isolation from the rest of the board.

The *finance committee* is typically chaired by the treasurer and is responsible for overseeing and reporting the financial aspects of the operation. This committee may make recommendations to the full board in matters such as financial procedures and controls, long-term investment, and debt management. The committee is also a useful group to advise on the creation and approval of yearly budgets.

The *nominating committee* identifies, interviews, and makes recommendations to the full board about potential trustees. As candidates are brought onto the board, this committee should also provide board orientation and review.

All other committees should be created as *ad hoc committees*, to address a particular goal or outcome. Once that goal has been reached, the committee can be dissolved, allowing its members to work on other tasks.

Other Board-Related Issues

MINIMUM BOARD CONTRIBUTIONS

The trustees should be required to contribute financially to the organization as part of their membership. Every fund-raising effort begins with the board of trustees. Vital to the success of fund-raising campaigns is the ability to state that the board has contributed 100%—that is, everyone on the board has made a personal contribution to the effort at hand. Without this support, the organization's development program operates on an unstable and suspect foundation. Board members are those people from the community who have a strong connection with the values and mission of the organization, and if these individuals do not contribute financially to the efforts of the organization, who else would?

The amount of money a board member is required to contribute to the organization should be relative to the size of the organization, its needs for financial donations, and the expectations of the board. Yearly minimum board contributions do not have to be a personal sacrifice. Board contributions can be as low as $5 or as high as necessary. One way to gauge a minimum gift amount is to base it on the total operating budget. For example, if an organization has a $1 million operating budget, is a minimum gift of $1,000 appropriate? That figure is 0.1% of the total budget. If the mission calls for a board that is economically diverse, the organization can reduce that amount to $500, or 0.05% of the total operating budget.

As the organization grows, the minimum donation should also increase. Five years in the future, if the organization discussed in the latter example above has doubled its budget, board members should be required to contribute $1,000 ($2,000,000 x 0.05%). Basing the minimum board gift on a percentage of overall budget allows the organization to increase board giving as the organization grows. Increases become automatic as the company develops and are not subject to the personal beliefs of current board members. It is very important that everyone on the board contributes something to the organization. Minimum donations set a clear expectation for board participation and send a strong message to the organization's other funders.

REQUIREMENTS OF BOARD MEMBERSHIP

Every organization must decide what responsibilities are required of its board members. Some are obvious, such as buying season tickets, attending meetings, participating in committee service, and bringing new people to the organization's activities (performances, events, and benefits). The requirements must be stated in writing, and a prospective trustee must agree to them in the cultivation process before being formally accepted to serve on the board.

Because changes to the bylaws have to be submitted to federal and state agencies, these extra requirements can be written in a supplemental document that is given to board members during the interview process. This document would state any and all board requirements that fall outside the typical scope of the bylaws. Because these requirements are not a part of the bylaws, changes can be made to them more freely and with less effort procedurally by the board and staff.

STAFF MEMBERS SERVING AS BOARD MEMBERS

Often executive staff members are required to attend board meetings as part of their job description. Although they attend these meetings and help provide information and guidance in the decision-making process, they are not usually allowed to vote. When hot issues arise, this practice can lead to resentment in the staff as well as a sense of disconnect between the staff and the board. Executive staff will also be less motivated to implement unfavorable directives of the board if they feel they did not have a say in the process. Hence, as Nello McDaniel and George Thorn state in their book *Arts Boards: Creating a New Community Equation*, "Staff leadership should have full voting membership on the board. The voting membership is a way to recognize that arts organizations are artistically centered and staff led. It is arts professionals in partnership with the board of trustees who must behave in a responsible, professional, and ethical manner" (1994, 49).

In order for staff to have the full board privileges and voting power, the voting staff members must also share full board responsibility, as it pertains to state law. There are a few extra responsibilities a staff member serving on the board must assume, the most obvious of which is making the minimum board contributions.

The Last Words on Boards

A lot of time has been given to discussing the role of the board and the principles that guide it. A healthy board is an essential element to a successful organization. A board that operates without proper structure or purpose can wreak havoc in an organization. Unfortunately, too few good examples exist for us to follow in the field, as is evident by the plethora of articles and books on the subject of nonprofit board management. It seems unfortunate that over the past twenty-five years the performing arts industry has not actively sought to revamp its board system. Rather, it has tried to cure the symptoms, not the cause. This is not to say that there are not a lot of good intentions on the part of board members, but rather that there is a lack of clear expectations and directions from managers. This is usually caused in part by a lack of foresight and long-term planning and by creating boards designed to serve the immediate needs of the organization rather than the organization's future needs.

The Operational Functions of an Arts Organization

*H*aving unique and clearly articulated mission and vision statements and creating an appropriate board are just the beginnings of a strong and vibrant organization. For companies to be successful, the values held within the mission and vision statements must be embedded in their day-to-day activities. Each organizational unit and each employee must share the common and agreed-upon values of the whole organization and focus on obtaining that outcome.

In addition to the workings of the board of trustees, the day-to-day operations of a nonprofit arts organization can be broken down into five basic areas:

1. fund-raising
2. marketing
3. production
4. finance
5. long-term planning

In an average nonprofit arts organization, the development department can be responsible for raising 40%

to 60% of the company's overall revenue. The development department naturally holds a place of great responsibility, with the department's successes and failures dramatically affecting every aspect of the organization.

Equal in responsibility to the development department is the marketing department. A majority of the remaining percentage of revenue—40% to 60%—falls within the jurisdiction of the marketing department. This department sells the organization's products and services. The marketing department's task is to bring audiences in to see the work of the company. While often it seems that companies are seeking new audience members, there should also be a focus on enhancing the relationship with current patrons.

The function of the production department is the implementation of the programs and services that are produced by the organization. These may include performances and productions, tours, classes, and outreach programs. This broad range of programming may have many subcategories, which might include costumes, props, carpentry, education, and so forth. What binds these groups together is that they are responsible for what the audience sees, which is the realization of the organization's values in an artistic environment.

The finance department has the responsibility of recording, monitoring, and planning the monetary transactions of the organization and issuing reports on the company's financial position. Part of the duties of the finance department include the preparation of the annual budget and the final annual audit. With the help of other departments and the organization's leadership, the finance department will translate organizational goals into a fiscal road map. In this way, budgeting and planning are closely tied.

Long-term planning is the formal process of understanding the opportunities and threats of the external environment and the strengths and weaknesses of the internal environment as well as determining what actions to take to best fulfill the organization's vision. In each of these areas the mission and the vision statements should guide the decision-making process and focus the organization on a future goal. The action of each unit affects the other units as well as the entire organization.

The following sections further explain the operational functions of arts management. Each section has been stripped of many of the theories and applications of these business areas to get to the essence of each and discover its direct correlation to the mission and vision statements. If the mission statement is an organization's measure of success and its vision statement its ultimate goal, then all operating decisions must comply with these statements. That is the principle of a mission-and-vision-centered approach to arts management.

Fund-Raising

It is widely known that approximately 80% of all donations in the United States are made by individuals. The remaining 20% are made through corporations, foundations, government agencies, and other granting organizations. These granting organizations make their philanthropic decisions through committees, individuals, or peer panel evaluation systems. Ultimately all contributions to nonprofit organizations are made by individuals.

People make donations to nonprofit organizations for a multitude of reasons. The prevailing reason people give money to a particular organization is because they share the same values and beliefs as the organization. An individual that contributes to the local orchestra may do so because he believes that a working orchestra is important within the community and he appreciates the type of work being produced by that company. The reason an individual might give to one orchestra and not another is because one organization is more closely aligned with the individual's own values and beliefs. Similarly, corporations, foundations, and granting organizations give contributions to those organizations that align with their corporate beliefs and cultures, as found in their granting guidelines.

People make charitable contributions for other personal reasons, such as to affirm a sense of community, to feel good or important about helping, to acknowledge their personal connections with the organization, and to answer a donation request. But no one would give to an organization if the core values of that organization did not agree with her own personal value system. Therefore, fund-raising is ultimately the communication of the organization's values and beliefs in a manner that will yield a positive response in the form of a donation from a potential donor. It is a sharing of ideas and principles.

All development campaigns should begin with a substantial amount of research. The research process involves the organization's development staff working through the names of individuals and organizations to determine how closely the values of the organization match those of each potential donor and what type and size of contribution a donor might be able to make. These potential donors are found within the company's ticket-buying population. Once a list of patrons has been generated, the staff will create opportunities to communicate the values of the organization so that the potential donor will recognize that both parties share common beliefs and that the organization is deserving of his financial support. The closer the pairing of values is between the potential donor and the organization, the greater the likelihood of a contribution.

The mechanisms for creating this dialogue include direct-mail campaigns, proposal and grant writing, face-to-face solicitation, and special events, to name a few. In each of these opportunities the development staff articulates the mission of the organization in a way that is understood by the potential donor and conveys the values and beliefs of the organization by describing the company's programs, successes, needs, and dreams of the future. If the organization is mission centered, each of the company's programs will demonstrate the organization's commitment to its mission and its vision. The expression of an organization's vision can be a useful tool in fund-raising. Articulating the organization's vision for the future can motivate potential donors to support the organization even though it has yet to bring its vision to fruition. Communicating the organization's vision to potential donors will serve to strengthen the case for support and indicate a sense of organizational direction.

For example, say a theatre troupe that tours throughout the region performing plays in the school system (kindergarten through high school) is raising money for its programs. The development department does its research and determines that there is a wide range of potential donors, including parents of the children seeing the shows, schoolteachers and administrators who value the program and hire the troupe to perform at their school, other theatregoers who believe in the value of the arts in the public school system, PTA groups, local foundations who give to arts-in-education programs, local businesses and corporations that cater to children or families with children, local companies who embrace community responsibility and support arts in education, government arts agencies, and others. In order to generate the most favorable response from the potential donor in each of these cases, the organization must match the potential donor with the proper method of solicitation and the proper rearticulation of the mission and vision statements. In each of these examples, the development department might highlight a particular area of the troupe's residency program that would most appeal to the values of the donor. In such a case the development department might focus on underserved population groups, preperformance lectures, study guides, or the particular issues that the plays might explore, such as premarital sex, HIV/AIDS, drug use, and so forth. While the organization is not altering its programming, it is trying to state that it shares common goals with the donor.

Unfortunately, successful fund-raising can also lead to potential problems. Particularly problematic to some organizations is the desire to raise contributed revenue at any cost. In such scenarios, a grant writer might create a program on paper that fits the guidelines and values of the granting organization but is outside the values of the receiving organization. If funding is received, the organization is obligated to implement that program, shifting the priorities and makeup of the organization's mission. Unconsciously the organization has moved away from its own beliefs and values to those of the granting organization. In the long term this error can be very costly. Once funding support is no longer available from the granting organization, the company is left with a program that lacks internal support and is financially draining to the organization.

Fund-raising is not a competition to see how much money the organization can raise from a particular source, but rather the creation of a partnership that allows both parties to fulfill their goals. Fund-raising is the process of forming and maintaining relationships. Fund-raisers recognize the need for a continuing relationship with their donors. The creation of understanding of and commitment to a particular purpose will lead to strong and continued financial support.

All fund-raising activities of an organization begin with the mission statement and the values held by the organization. All of the development staff's research, planning, and implementation is directed by the mission and vision of the organization. When speaking to current and potential donors, by staying true and consistent in the articulation of the mission, the organization has the potential to build lasting and rewarding relationships with its donors. Fundraising is a three- to five-year process, and like the formation of any relationship, it involves building trust, sharing experiences, and understanding. If the relationship is built on firm ground, then the rewards of that relationship are unlimited.

Marketing

Marketing for the performing arts goes beyond the idea of selling goods and services to a target market. Communicating the values and beliefs of the organization to a potential audience is essential to a long-term marketing strategy. Unlike commercial producers that market only one show or production at a time, a nonprofit performing arts organization is the sum of many different products and programs. In this way the name and goodwill of the company has more lasting power than a particular program or production. While a company may receive both favorable and unfavorable audience reactions to a particular work it presents, the company itself is judged by the sum of many experiences.

When people make decisions about using one product over another, they often consider the company behind the product. Whether or not they are familiar with that company and have had good prior experiences with its products is part of the evaluation process. Similarly, if you bought a car from a particular manufacturer and had a bad experience, you would be hesitant to purchase another car from that company even if it was a different model. A particularly bad experience with a company is not likely to be forgotten. When marketing performing arts, the organization must first market the institution by expressing its values and beliefs. Individual products are sold through the larger ideal and perceived values of the organization.

Marketing functions in very much the same way as fundraising; it is responsible for communicating organizational values to a potential market. And, like fund-raising, marketing must begin with research and planning. Market research includes examining the environment of the community that the organization serves. Central to any marketing plan is the concept of positioning. Philip Kotler and Joanne Scheff, in their book *Standing Room Only: Strategies for Marketing the Performing Arts*, define positioning as "the act of designing the organization's image and offer so that it occupies a distinct and valued place in the target customer's minds. Positioning involves (1) creating a real differentiation and (2) making it known to others" (1997, 115).

How does an organization determine what makes it different from other companies? The answer is within the organization's mission statement. By definition, a good mission statement is unique and appropriate only for one organization. It is the responsibility of the marketing department to communicate to the potential market the uniqueness of the organization through its marketing campaigns. Marketing becomes about celebrating what makes an organization distinctive, and while there are countless marketing vehicles to choose from, the message is always the same: "Our mission makes us one of a kind." As such, marketing is the rearticulation of the mission statement to a target market.

The marketing department serves as a communicator to the general public. Patrons attend performances because they share similar beliefs and values with the organization. The organization makes a product that the patrons value. In theatre, specific organizational values could take the form of Shakespearean, modern, avant-garde, or musical theatre. People who do not attend the organization's events either do not agree with its values or have yet to be convinced that their values are in line with the organization's values. In order to change these nonattendees into patrons, the marketing staff must understand how best to communicate the mission of the organization to them.

As an example, let's say a company has decided to produce *The Three Sisters*, by Anton Chekhov. If it is a community theatre and providing roles for local actors is a part of the mission, it may wish to list the names of the local actors who are taking part in the production to highlight community participation. A theatre might also list the actors' names if its mission is about providing professional quality productions. By listing the actors' names or by using the phrase *starring* or *featuring*, the company is marketing the fact that it has high-caliber professionals acting in the production. Promoting the actors sends a message that is unique to the organization. If the mission is to produce the great classics of theatre, the decision to produce *The Three Sisters* was an obvious one. Marketing in this scenario would focus on what makes *The Three Sisters* a classic. If the mission is to promote the work of new playwrights, highlighting the fact that this is a new translation by an emerging playwright would be central to the company's marketing efforts. Of course, any of these types of theatre companies can advertise the show in all of these ways, but the company's reason for producing the play should be the primary marketing thrust.

The methods used to market the organization should also relate to the mission. If the mission is about serving a younger audience, the marketing department may rely more heavily on the Internet and technology. A more classic theatre might rely on classic forms of advertising such as newspapers, magazines, and direct mail. A popular theatre may choose to use radio and television as its main sources of communication. In each of these scenarios, the marketing staff is asking: How might the organization best get its product information across to the target audience? The answer to this question helps the staff determine the best marketing vehicles by which to communicate the mission of the organization to the target market.

Marketing the cultural arts is expressing the organizational values and beliefs to a potential market. Because personal values shape consumers' decisions, it is critical that an organization consistently articulate its mission to the potential market in order for the audience to identify with the products and participate in the organization's services over the long term. Creating different marketing values for each product or production offered by a particular organization will leave the market confused.

For far too long cultural organizations have sold each offering as a separate product from the whole. They have done so to try to increase new audiences, selecting different target markets for different productions. When patrons are sold one set of values and beliefs, they are dissatisfied when they come back to experience another offering and find that the values system has changed. Marketing in the performing arts is not so much about building new audiences as it is about developing a loyal, likeminded audience that frequently uses the organization's services. It is considerably more expensive to attract a new customer into the organization than it is to reach someone who already uses the company's products.

Production

The area referred to as production in this section is meant to include all of a company's goods and services or, in the case of the performing arts, all of its performance series, outreach programs, tours, classes, and so forth. Production consists of all activities performed by a company from which it generates revenue or receives funding support.

When thinking of production within the context of an artistic institution, you cannot help but think of making art. The production or the creation of art can be affected by many influences, such as the artists' training, values, and beliefs as well as the community in which the art is to be created. Performing arts companies are founded on particular artistic principles—ideals that should be clearly articulated within the mission statement. Every artistic program should reflect that mission statement, whether it is a main-stage production, an educational program, or a studio presentation. If the artistic programming is not consistent it will cause customer confusion. The ideal organization is one in which patrons move freely from product to product with a common understanding of the values held by the organization.

As an example, consider a theatre company that produces new works. The concept of "new works" is defined in the mission statement to mean plays that were written within the last ten years. Over the past several seasons, the company has experienced modest financial growth and artistic success. However, the company still cannot afford to employ the full-time staff that it needs to take full advantage of funding and marketing opportunities. Over time, the idea of producing *A Christmas Carol* is brought up at staff meetings and board meetings. No other theatre in the area produces *A Christmas Carol*, and it seems like a sure thing for increasing revenues and audience size, which would enable the organization to hire the staff it needs to produce the type of work it desires. What should it do?

The obvious thing to consider is how this production of *A Christmas Carol* will fit with the mission. The play fails to meet the criteria of the mission statement because it was not written within the last ten years; however, the adaptation the company is considering has been written within the past ten years. Therefore the organization may have to explore more deeply its values and beliefs, which might be found in an artistic statement. The issue to explore is: Why do we produce only plays written in the past ten years? Is it because the company seeks to promote and develop new playwrights, in which case a new adaptation of an old text may apply, or is it to produce plays that explore modern man and society, in which case this play would not apply? In either case the company is asking its mission: Can the organization produce this show?

If in this example the company produces new plays because they reflect modern social issues, then a production of *A Christmas Carol* in the classic presentation falls outside its mission. If the organization went ahead with the show regardless of its mission, then the company would begin to serve two separate audiences. One audience would come for *A Christmas Carol* and a separate audience would see its new works. Ultimately, this type of programming leads to audience confusion and to confusion of purpose within the company. This kind of programming also causes problems for the marketing and development departments because they would no longer be able to use the mission statement for the basis of their message, for it would not be applicable for both audiences. A possible solution for the company would be to find a holiday script that would accomplish the same fiscal and ticket-sales goals as *A Christmas Carol* but that was written in the past ten years. Another option for the company would be to create a separate organization for the sole purpose of producing an annual production of *A Christmas Carol*, of which all proceeds would be donated to the parent theatre company. In this scenario the mission of the parent company would be separate from that of the new organization and would therefore create managerial clarity when making decisions for either enterprise.

When a company begins to make decisions about the type of programs it seeks to produce, it must weigh these choices against the mission and vision statements. It must ask the questions: How does this program fulfill our mission statement? and How does it move our company closer to its vision? These questions must be answered in relation to all existing and new programs throughout the operation. Without this type of constant evaluation, the productions of the company may move away from its central purpose. When the productions fall out of line with the mission and vision statement, so too does the entire organization.

In the performing arts community a common art-versus-business conversation is: Has the business of running a performing arts organization overshadowed the artistic purpose of the organization? The conversation should not be about art versus administration, but rather the mission statement above all else because the mission statement is the combination of art and business.

Finance

The financial operation of an organization consists of many different components, including bookkeeping, cost controls, cash flow, debt and investment management, and budgeting. This discussion focuses on the budgetary process because it is the fiscal process that dictates the flow of the operation. The budget ultimately serves as the principal financial goal of the organization. The budgetary process serves as a short-term planning tool, setting the financial goals for an organization.

Each year the finance staff begins the process of budgeting for the next fiscal year. A budget is created based on a variety of internal and external sources: current revenues and expenses, economic conditions, product selection, social trends, and staffing needs. These factors all play a part in the budget process. The task of creating a budget for an organization can be described as the allocation of resources based on organizational priorities. Organizations have a limited amount of resources that are allocated for use by each department or program (financial, staffing, equipment, and so forth). The most effective way to prepare a budget for a nonprofit organization is through its departments and programs. Each program should be broken down into a separate budget to demonstrate that program's direct and indirect expenses. Creating program budgets that are smaller slices of the larger operational budget gives management a more focused view of a particular area or program as well as the ability to set individual financial objectives for each of the areas.

During the budgetary process each of the programs is broken down by its direct revenues and direct expenses; these are the line items that can be directly attributed to a certain program. If you remove the program from the budget, you can remove these associated expenses and revenues. Program budgets include all marketing, development, and facility expenses directly related to the production of the particular program or service. Expenses that cannot be directly attributed to a particular program would be considered indirect expenses or overhead. In the case of indirect expenses, some mechanism should be devised to approximate each program's use of that expense or revenue. When the group has completed the program budget, the organization should have accounted for 100% of the program's revenues and expenses. Once this process is complete, the organization will have a clear understanding of which programs are financially successful and which are not. In other words, which programs have been budgeted to generate a surplus?

However, a financial surplus is not the overriding measure of success when working with a nonprofit organization. The measure of success comes from the fulfillment of the mission statement. Two more important questions to ask are: Which of these programs is most closely aligned with the company's mission? and Which program is moving the organization closer to its vision? In times of severe fiscal crisis or economic turndown, an organization may be forced to make drastic operational cuts. In order to bring a budget into a balanced situation the organization will need to ask: What is the minimum level of programming the organization requires to fulfill its mission? Even in fiscally healthy times it is appropriate to ask these questions: Why do we have this program? How does it serve the mission? and How does it advance the organization toward its vision? In this scenario we are ranking programs not on how much money they generate for the company, but rather on how well they serve the mission of the organization.

Through this type of financial analysis, the company can begin to make clear decisions about which programs need additional resources to be successful. Or, in some cases, it helps the company determine which programs need to be eliminated because their poor performance is affecting the performance of other programs, thus reducing the success of the whole organization.

If the decision is made to pull a weak program from the budget, the program budget should be reworked so that indirect expenses are reallocated. The remaining programs will have to absorb the overhead costs that were once charged to the eliminated program. Reallocation alters the entire organization's budget as well as each program's finances. This type of thinking and evaluation helps clarify the purpose of the financial planning process and, while it is time-consuming, there will be fewer surprises for the organization throughout the fiscal year.

Long-Term Planning

To some, planning for a nonprofit organization seems like a waste of time. With so many other important things to be done, who has time to plan? Because the organization wades through the budgeting process each year, isn't that enough?

With the world changing so quickly, what is the use of planning? However, long-term planning should be an important part of an organization's ongoing operational procedures and practices. It is critical that an arts organization think about its future, its vision. Long-term planning allows the organization to test short-term decisions against the future implications for the organization.

People are hesitant about beginning a long-term or strategic planning process in an organization for many reasons. They are afraid of change and the loss of control that planning may cause, they are afraid that it will take up too much of their time or cost the organization money that should be going to its programs, or they may feel that planning has never been successful for the organization. None of these reasons should overshadow the benefits of planning. The time and energy an organization invests now in the planning process will have a beneficial effect on the future health of the organization. Planning is not a one-time obligation, but should be a consistent and ongoing function of the organization. As planning becomes ingrained, the process will become more efficient and more successful.

"Strategic planning is the means used to consider future operations and make decisions about organizational direction. Strategic planning provides a perspective for the review of mission, goals, objectives, and programs and the related use of resources"(Turk and Gallo 1984, 22). Long-term planning is the process of examining the external environment in which an organization operates as well as its internal environment to determine how best to align the two for the further success of the organization's mission and vision. If an organization has thoughtfully constructed its mission and vision statements, then that organization should be well on its way to successful and meaningful long-term planning. Organizations use the planning process to take advantage of the environment and to find opportunities to advance their mission and move closer to their vision.

An organization can conduct its planning process in a variety of ways, but the process should involve the following:

- acknowledging the organization's mission and vision and the goals that emerge from them

- evaluating the opportunities and threats of the external environment—those forces that are outside the organization but affect its operation
- evaluating the strengths and weaknesses of the internal environment—those forces that are directly related to the running of the operation
- establishing organizational priorities and creating the systems in which goals will be met
- delegating authority over the systems and allocating the necessary resources for success

Long-term planning extends the visual horizon of the organization, but the same rules of values and beliefs apply. In planning, the focus of the organization is expanded to include the external environment and how that affects the operation of the organization. Planning asks the organization to implement the systems it needs to take advantage of the current environment or, in the case of economic decline, to protect itself from the external forces. One can begin to see how effective strategic planning can easily flow into the rest of the organization, making short-term planning more efficient and effective.

The most common mistake in the planning process is to be fixated upon the final report. The planning process is not about the final document, but rather the discovery of questions and problems; then the planner can develop strategies to overcome these obstacles. The process of planning should reveal to the organization the path or paths the organization needs to be on to reach its vision. It is an organizational call to action.

As the social and economic environment changes, so too must the organization. Programs that were essential and viable five years ago may no longer be appropriate for the organization or the community. Demographics could shift in such a way that the organization must make adjustments in its operations in order to continue. In extreme cases it may be determined that given the conditions of the external environment, it is no longer possible for the organization to continue. An important first question to ask during every planning session is: Given the current and future outlook for the external and internal environments, should this organization continue operations? Too often this question is overlooked or ignored, leading organizations and staff into decline and hardship. No one said that the organization would last forever, and no one can guarantee that in the future the mission will be as important and essential to the community as it is today. If the organization no longer serves its original mission or the long-term economic climate cannot sustain the organization, the leadership of that organization must prepare to cease operations so that it will avoid uncontrollable debt and distress to the staff. On the other hand, if an organization has carefully examined the external and internal environments, has determined that the mission and vision of the organization are still viable and important to the community, and has determined that the economic conditions do not warrant closure, then the organization can proceed with confidence and assurance that its planning process will result in the best possible situation for that organization.

Long-term planning is the process of plotting out goals and objectives that pertain to the mission statement and the vision statement of the organization in relation to the external and internal environments. The process of strategic planning helps create unity among staff members. The more people involved in the process and the more understanding and agreement for the proposed plan, the more likely the plan will be successful. Strategic planning helps the organization plot out measurable steps to best achieve its mission and vision, and it carefully and objectively examines the external and internal environments of the organization to identify weaknesses, opportunities, threats, and strengths. The planning committee objectively inventories each of the organization's programs to ensure they serve the central purpose, establishes organizational focus by setting priorities, and builds support among stakeholders.

Management and Leadership | 5

*A*s Peter Drucker once proclaimed, management is doing things right—improving operational performance, maximizing revenues, and reducing expenses while increasing artistic production values and audience appreciation. Leadership is doing the right things—setting organizational priorities and allocating human and fiscal resources to fulfill the organization's vision.

The organization's mission and vision statements come alive through the examples set by the leadership of the organization. It is extremely difficult to get a large group of people to agree on a single statement, but that is exactly the task of the leadership. Leaders are at the helm to show employees the way, to keep them on track, to show them the errors in their ways, and to reward them when appropriate. They create organizational focus, delegate authority, and empower employees. Mission and vision statements should function intuitively in the mind of the leader. It should be second nature to the leader to always act in accordance with the mission and to always keep the vision foremost in his mind.

Nonprofit groups often form around a single strong leader or a core group whose vision and energy influence every aspect of the organization's actions. Yet, if the organization is to mature, the founding leader must delegate authority and responsibility of the organization. This can be accomplished by ingraining the values and beliefs of the organization in everyone's mind through the use of mission and vision statements and turning over leadership responsibility to more and more employees, empowering them to take ownership of the organization as did the founding leaders in the beginning of the organization's history.

When a founding leader leaves an organization, it is vital that the organization has institutionalized its values and beliefs. An arts institution that has a strong mission and a clear vision as well as a strategic plan in place can better weather leadership changes without being swayed from its original purpose. Organizations that are not secure are likely to reinvent themselves as they take on a new leader and that leader's vision. This change is not necessarily negative, but it will have an initial adverse effect on the organization as previous stakeholders move away from the company. The ideal organization is one in which the change of leadership does not alter the operation of the organization.

A leader of an organization is the keeper of the vision, the communicator of organizational values and beliefs, and the person who sets institutional priorities and allocates organizational resources. The leader does this to create change that positively affects the organization. The leader's priority is to reach the organization's vision, and the leader's strategic priorities are the two or three long-term goals found within the planning process that will have the greatest impact on moving the organization closer to its vision. In the budgetary and strategic planning process, not only does the leader ensure proper funding and support for the strategic priorities, but she also delegates appropriate authority and responsibility. Leaders understand the importance and power of delegating authority and the creation of secondary leaders within a company. Leaders are tireless promoters of the organization's purpose and actions.

Conclusion

In a simple equation a mission statement can be formulated as follows:

> organizational values + organizational beliefs =
> mission statement

And a vision statement can be stated as follows:

> mission statement + time (in years) = vision statement

It is that simple to remember. The mission statement is a tool for the manager and the vision statement is a leadership tool. And, in one way or another, all of the organization's activities center on the mission and vision statements. Marketing is the function of differentiating a company's product from another company's products by communicating that product's uniqueness to the market and sharing product values with a target market. All of these functions are contained within the organizational mission statement. So, too, is the function of fund-raising. Fund-raising is the process of finding donors with similar values as the company and matching values to specific company programs. Budgeting, like planning, is a process of allocating the company's resources to fulfill the organization's mission and vision.

If a program or activity does not serve these statements, it does not serve the company. It is that simple.

Obviously a lot has been left unsaid. If you have not already done so, you should utilize other books that expand on the concepts and principles of board management, fund-raising principles and practices, marketing techniques and methods, planning methods, and leadership principles. As you do read other books, keep the principles of this book in mind and continually ask yourself: How do these new principles apply to the mission and vision of my organization? How can I use this information to communicate to my stakeholders the values and beliefs of my organization? Do these techniques honor the values set forth in the organizational mission statement and vision statement?

While it is easy to write down and understand the principles contained within this book, it is more difficult to implement and maintain them. If running an organization following a mission-and-vision-centered approach were simple, everyone would do it. The people who become great leaders and create great organizations work on achieving their goals every day. Success is a long-term prospect. If when following this process you falter, get back on track and start again.

Bibliography and Other Suggested Readings

Ball, William. 1984. *A Sense of Direction: Some Observations on the Art of Directing*. New York: Drama Publishers. (ISBN 0-89676-082-0.)

Bennis, Warren, and Burt Nanus. 1985. *Leaders: The Strategies for Taking Charge*. New York: Harper & Row. (ISBN 0-06-015246-X.)

Clurman, Harold. 1961. *The Fervent Years: The Story of the Group Theatre and the Thirties*. New York: Alfred A. Knopf. (ISBN 0-30680-186-8)

Covey, Stephen. 1989. *The 7 Habits of Highly Effective People*. New York: Simon & Schuster. (ISBN 0-671-70863-5.)

Dow, Roger, and Susan Cook. 1996. *Turned On: Eight Vital Insights to Energize Your People, Customers, and Profits*. New York: HarperBusiness. (ISBN 0-88730-766-3.)

Drucker, Peter F. 1974. *Management: Tasks, Responsibilities, Practices*. New York: Harper & Row. (ISBN 0-06-011092-9.)

Hall, Peter. 1999. *The Necessary Theatre*. New York: Theatre Communications Group. (ISBN 1-55936-178-6.)

Hesselbein, Frances, Marshall Goldsmith, Richard Beckhard, eds. 1996. *The Leader of the Future: New Visions, Strategies, and Practices for the Next Era.* San Francisco: Jossey-Bass. (ISBN 07879-0935-1.)

Hopkins, Karen, and Carolyn Friedman. 1997. *Successful Fundraising for Arts and Cultural Organizations.* Phoenix, AZ: Oryx. (ISBN 1-57356-029-4.)

Kotler, Philip, and Joanne Scheff. 1997. *Standing Room Only: Strategies for Marketing the Performing Arts.* Boston: Harvard Business School Press. (ISBN 0-87584-737-4.)

McDaniel, Nello, and George Thorn. 1991. *The Quiet Crisis in the Arts.* New York: ARTS Action Issues. (ISBN 1-884345-03-04.)

———. 1994. *Arts Boards: Creating a New Community Equation.* New York: ARTS Action Issues. (ISBN 1-884345-03-04.)

New York State Legislature. February 20, 2004. Not-for-Profit Corporation Law. Accessed from http://public.leginfo.state.ny.us/frmload.cgi?MENU-28753919.

Peters, Thomas, and Robert Waterman Jr. 1982. *In Search of Excellence: Lessons from America's Best Run Companies.* New York: Warner. (ISBN 0-446-38281-7.)

Rowe, Alan J., Richard O. Mason, Karl E. Dickel, and Neil H. Snyder. 1986. *Strategic Management: A Methodological Approach.* Boston: Addison Wesley. (ISBN 0-201-15736-5.)

Setterberg, Fred, and Kary Schulman. 1985. *Beyond Profit: The Complete Guide to Managing the Nonprofit Organization.* New York: Harper & Row. (ISBN 0-06-015472-1.)

Turk, Fredrick, and Robert Gallo. 1984. *Financial Management Strategies for Arts Organizations.* New York: ACA. (ISBN 0-915400-41-3.)

Voss, Zannie Giraud, and Glenn B. Voss. 2000. "Exploring the Impact of Organizational Values and Strategic Orientation on Performance in Not-for-Profit Professional Theatre." *The International Journal of Arts Management* 3: 62–75.